Be

Autobiography of
Ruth Taylor Williams

The Warmth of Home

by

Ruth Taylor Williams

Ruth Williams

ISBN 978-1508644279

Front Cover Photo by Sheri Perenon
Back Cover Photo by Martin Erickson
Cover Design by Dan Erickson

Contents

Part IV:

"The Warmth of Home... Besides Mealtimes!" 77

Conclusion: "My Challenge to You"........................... 114

Epilogue 117

Thanks... 118

Notes 120

Foreword

Psalm 113:5-8

"Who is like the Lord our God,
the One who sits enthroned on high,
who stoops down to look
on the heavens and the earth?
He raises the poor from the dust
and lifts the needy from the ash heap.
He seats them with princes,
with the princes of their people."

The stories now being written of our lives are oftentimes stories for later. Sometimes our stories have to sit and settle and sink into the fabric of ongoing life before they are meant to be told. Sometimes stories need to be saved and aged before they will be received or can have their most powerful effect. Our life stories are being written, revised and edited. One day they will finally be prepared for others to read or hear. One day, perhaps when we are older, perhaps when we are gone, God will use the stories of our lives to make a difference in someone else's life.

My mother is now ninety-eight. The time is here to share her story in print. How grateful she would be to know that her story could help make a difference in your life.

- Connie Snyder

Prologue

We have all become familiar with the impassioned proclamation by Martin Luther King, "I have a dream!" I recently read, "The dreamers are the saviors of the world." As a dreamer, I would be a savior of the Christian home! My dream is to kindle a flame on the hearth of many homes to bring warmth and love, and the invitation to "come on in and enjoy!" I always wanted my home to be a place where my husband loved to return each day and find his personal needs met with love and understanding. I wanted my children to gravitate to it with a desire to see me, their room, and their gathered memories as their lives marched from one stage to another. I wanted home to be a place where they felt wanted, loved, and comforted from anything "out there" that had bothered or troubled them. I wanted a home that was a refuge—a haven—a bit of heaven to go to heaven in.

Though we know so little about Jesus' earthly home, we are certain He could not forget the wondrous memory of His Heavenly Father's home. After spending the years necessary to show His love for us and accomplish the work of His earth walk, He "went back home" to His Father's house. He was received with open arms, angels singing, and a great celebration! I always wanted my home and its atmosphere to be like that for my family, as well as for others who came to our house.

Some might wonder why I have felt compelled to write my thoughts concerning home and what I could share that would be of help, inspiration and encouragement to someone else. For most of my life, I had not thought such a thing possible.

An idea was born in me through a little story I read in Ted Engstrom's forceful book, **The Pursuit of Excellence**. It goes like this:

> *An American Indian tells about a brave who found an eagle's egg and put it into the nest of a prairie chicken. The eaglet hatched with the brood of chicks and grew up with them.*
>
> *All his life, the changeling eagle, thinking he was a prairie chicken, did what the prairie chickens did. He scratched in the dirt for seeds and insects to eat. He clucked and cackled. And he flew in a brief thrashing of wings and flurry of feathers no more than a few feet off the ground. After all, that's how prairie chickens were supposed to fly.*

Years passed. And the changeling eagle grew very old. One day, he saw a magnificent bird far above him in the cloudless sky. Hanging with graceful majesty on the powerful wind currents, it soared with scarcely a beat of its strong golden wings.

"What a beautiful bird!" said the changeling eagle to his neighbor. "What is it?"

"That's an eagle—the chief of the birds," the neighbor clucked. "But don't give it a second thought. You could never be like him."

So the changeling eagle never gave it another thought. And it died thinking it was a prairie chicken.

What a tragedy. Built to soar into the heavens, but conditioned to stay earthbound, he pecked at stray seeds and chased insects. Though designed to be among the most awesome of all fowl, instead, he believed his neighbor's counsel: "Hey, you're only a prairie chicken... Come on, let's go find us some insects."[1]

I must confess, this has been my attitude. You see, I was a prairie chicken. And I believed the counsel that I could never be anything else. This is my story and "where ah come from."

Part I: "Where Ah Come From"

I was born a little Okie. I have never liked that term (though it may mean different things to different people). To me, it carried with it a certain stigma associated with the very poor and migrant people of the south. But that is what my family became through all my childhood. My parents were Cyrus Walker and Maybelle Taylor. My oldest sister, Katie, died in infancy. Then came Clara, Shelton, Hazel, Ruth (that's me), and Joe. We were an itinerant family from Frederick, Oklahoma. We were always looking for a new sighting of an oasis or the promise of a better living farther down the dusty roads. In this searching process, we always came short of the dream. The jobs were always temporary, consisting of farm work, clearing land of mesquite bushes, grubbing out stumps, sawing wood, working in the cotton fields plantin' cotton, choppin' cotton, and later pickin' cotton. At this time we did not really have a home anywhere. Our whole life was like camping out. We lived in tents and traveled in a covered wagon.

*

"Unexpected Turn: Sister Clara"

In my childish memory I still recall some strange and sad things that befell us, and others like us, in our way of life. For years and years we never talked about these things and kept them locked securely as "skeletons in the closet." I will tell you a pitiable story of something that took place during this period that affected our lives deeply forever after.

We struck up an acquaintance with another family with eight children in similar circumstances. I will only briefly tell you about the man in this family. His name was Jack and he was about thirty-five years old. Over time, this man took a shine to my fifteen year-old sister, Clara. One day they left camp on some proposed errand, and they never returned. We were so poor, and not knowing how to follow the situation, nothing was done to retrieve the wandering pair. A woman and her eight children were deserted, and our family was devastated by the turn of events. For five long years we had no word or idea of what had happened to them. The only thing we could do was move on.

*

"Alligator Scare"

When I was about five years old, my dad was offered a job to build a sawmill. This took us to East Texas, down by the Natches River. We lived in an old log cabin that was infested with spiders, scorpions, blister bugs and other mini-monsters that could cause trouble to unsuspecting children. Though I was very young, there are two things that I remember about living there. One was when I was bitten by some kind of bug. One bite was on my leg and the other next to my left eye. Mother treated them with some home remedy. The bites finally healed, but left scars that I carry to this day.

The other thing I remember was the day we went down by the river for a picnic. Have you ever seen how alligators crawl up on the banks of rivers, take a little nap, sun themselves, and then slide back into the water, leaving a slide for another time of rest? Well, I was playing too closely to one of these slides. I started to slip down the slide and into the alligator-infested river. My mother saw me just in the knick of time! She grabbed my clothes and was able to pull me back up to safety. Whew! What a close call!

I was saved from becoming a juicy morsel for those fierce, hungry alligators. My little mother came to the rescue!

As it turned out, the work at the sawmill came to a halt for my father because he contracted malaria and almost died. My mother's brother and my dad's brother came to our rescue and took my very sick father and the rest of our family back to our home town, Frederick, Oklahoma. It was a trying experience for all of us. This was but one of several times we had to be rescued from some disastrous happening along our way of life.

*

"In the Black of Midnight"

Ever looking for work, my dad stopped at a farmhouse one day to ask the man who lived there if he might need a hired hand. He was hired! Dad was so pleased to have a job. He plunged into the work assigned to him. I was enrolled at a little one-room schoolhouse to begin first grade. We seemed all set. Mother was given a job helping the wife of the man who had hired my dad. I don't know how long this lasted, but one night we were aroused from sleep, and were cautioned to be very quiet. My folks quickly got all our things together, pulled up stakes, and mysteriously left. As we passed the little schoolhouse, Mother left my schoolbooks on the steps. We were on our way. I asked my mother why we left the books there. She said, "We might get into trouble if we kept them." That's all that was ever said.

For many, many years this was not spoken about or referred to. Then, one day when I was visiting my sister, Hazel, in Oklahoma City, we found ourselves reminiscing about our days on the prairie. I asked her about the mysterious move that night long ago. She told me about the whole episode. The man who had hired my dad had propositioned my mother (on the q-tee) to see if she would be his mistress. She said she would think about it. She thought about it all right. She told my dad! This spurred him to have us stealthily leave camp in the black of midnight. This told the whole story. Whew! Am I ever glad my dad took the way out of this immoral situation. Here was just another event that pushed us to be "on the road again..."

*

"Our Little House on the Prairie"

Drifting along with the "tumbling tumbleweeds," we finally found our destination on the plains of West Texas. We took up residence on the prairies in a homestead government program. We always struggled in a determined effort to make things go. Success always eluded us. There were no buildings on the land. We lived in a homemade covered wagon until we made our first addition to the land. It was a one-room half-dugout, with bare sod for the floor and half of the wall. Over this was built the rest of the wall and a shingle roof. They used to say we lived like prairie dogs—just under the ground. This was our "Little House on the Prairie" and where I attended school through the rest of my childhood years in another one-room schoolhouse. There was no hope for any change of our existence.

As kids, we did all the western and pioneer type of activities. Some of these included collecting rattles from the rattlesnakes we killed, playing with dangerous tarantulas the size of a man's hand, listening to coyote packs howling at night, trapping and shooting small animals such as prairie dogs, jack rabbits, cotton tails, and birds. We rode horses, worked in the fields, and helped with home canning. We ate cornbread and molasses, and black eyed peas with relish called chow-chow. Our water was hauled in two barrels on a homemade sled pulled by an old horse from down the road a piece. Our fuel for the little wood burning stove was corn cobs and cow chips. These were sun baked, white cow chips which we gathered and threw onto a flatbed wagon. Hazel drove the horse and wagon. Joe and I gathered the cow chips, tossing them on the wagon until it was full. Then we would take them home and stack them like wood on the side of the dugout. We each had our own chores. It took all of us to make life livable.

Our modern convenience bathroom facility was a decorative outhouse made of gunny sacks stretched over poles. Our only toilet paper was a Sears Roebuck catalogue. Our only refrigerator was the cold, damp, sod floor under the bed. Somehow, we made it. We had to.

*

"Lost on the Prairie"

In our homesteading efforts on the Great Plains of West Texas, we could see for miles and miles around us. The prairie sprouted mesquite (sagebrush) bushes, blue grass, and many different kinds of cactus. Between our one-room country schoolhouse and our one-room dugout, which we called home, was a windmill and a large watering tank for cattle.

One day I had permission to stay after school to play with my fourth grade classmate, Laverne, who lived close to the school about two miles from my home. She and her family also lived in a dugout, but it was much nicer than ours. In fact, I thought it was luxurious. They had a wood floor on which was a carpet, and much nicer furniture than our built-in bed and homemade table and benches. I thought it was a step up in the world to be able to go there.

This one afternoon I was having so much fun with Laverne. Unaware of the time, however, I stayed too long. When I realized this, I struck out across the prairie alone. After walking some distance, I became afraid. Out there all alone, I sat down to rest and tried to get my bearings. I kept looking for the windmill. As I sat there on the ground, I did not think of possible rattlesnakes or other creeping, small animals, but fixed my eyes on the cactus all across my view. You may have seen, in other states, the various cactus with their weird and unique shapes. As I sat there, I noticed one cactus quite a distance away. I fancied that it was a little man. He was swinging one arm as he walked toward me; the other arm was missing. He sported a top hat. It seemed he was ever moving in my direction. Anytime I moved, he would move also. I became petrified and immobile out there in the now darkening sky. I didn't know what on earth to do. I winced at what could happen to me when my gaze was diverted for a moment. Coming across the prairie was a human form, that of a woman. It was my MOTHER coming to look for me. She was an angel! I will never forget the sight as my eyes filled with tears. In fact, they are filled with tears just now, thinking about her rescuing me at that moment of terror. The little man with this top hat never caught up with me, but my little, loving and concerned mother did! Though she never new what a poignant experience that was for me, it is a memory of her I will always treasure.

I must confess I did not always appreciate my parents. I thought of them as forever poor, not school educated, and being brought up without social graces. They didn't have resources to dress well or "fix up." These things really affected me in certain periods of my life. Thank God, I now have a bigger picture of their lives and influence on me and my brothers and sisters. The truth is that they were always hardworking, honest people, never in debt, never complainers. They accepted life as it came, with all its hardships, disappointments, heartaches and sadness.

Aside from these realities in their lives, there were some interesting sidelights that we smile about as we recall our way of life through the years. My dad used to sing old cowboy and western songs. He also quoted many-versed poems. My mother also loved to sing in her southern way. She sang old hymns and gospel songs. I learned many of them from her. She was a very friendly person, having no inhibitions about meeting anybody or talking to them as if they were old friends who loved and understood each other.

I have learned through many years of experience that it is not the outward, visual things about people (particularly my parents) that are so overwhelmingly important. It is the true person inside that makes someone real, acceptable, worthy of honor, respect and love.

I wish I had thought of these things much earlier in life, and had shared them with my hardworking dad and caring, loving mother. She was an angel of protection for me through many of the incidents in my life that could have been disastrous. Why is it we wait so long to realize the worth of accepting and appreciating the good in others, and instead, tend to dwell on the things we thought were to our disadvantage? I am still learning these lessons of seeing true value in others... and expressing it to them.

> *"Ve get too soon oldt,*
> *Undt too late schmart."*

*

"My Hero: Brother Shelton"

My oldest brother, Shelton, was one I always looked up to. He was nine years older than me. He worked with my dad on the various projects around our little compound and entered into all the jobs associated with the cotton field. He was a good worker. Dad built a shed that doubled for a cottonseed house and a room for my brother. Shelton slept on the cottonseed with two quilts as his bedding. The other half was a little room for him, his private space, his personal shelter.

There was a young preacher who came to our country church. He made friends with my brother and had a good influence on him, teaching him the importance of reading the Bible, of which he became an avid reader. I observed this and thought it would be nice to do the same.

One day I stayed home from school to help my mother do some canning. She wanted to do something for me in return and gave me a dollar for helping her. I told her I wanted to have a Bible so I could be like my brother. She sent for one from the Sears Roebuck catalogue. When it came I was so proud that I could now read it for myself. I must admit I could not understand it, but I read it night after night, and kept it safe under my pillow.

As Shelton got into his teen years, he decided he had had enough of prairie life and wanted to leave home. He unceremoniously jumped the fence Dad had made to keep out the small prairie animals, and started off alone on foot down the dusty road. I'll never forget that day. I watched him as long as I could see him. I cried and cried. He was my hero.

His dusty road brought him to Roswell, New Mexico, where he finally settled. We didn't hear from him much after that, but for years he was faithful to send me little gifts for my birthday. I loved him so much.

*

"The Girl With the Rose-Tinted Glasses: Sister Hazel"

Hazel always called me her "little sister." No, not her "kid" sister, but her "little sister," always spoken in her soft, southern voice. We always loved and admired each other. I had great reason to admire her, but it always baffled me that she had complimentary things to say about me. I wondered if she could have truly meant them.

My best and most memorable associations with Hazel were the years we spent out on the plains of West Texas. Hazel, being the go-getter that she always was, drove us in a horse-drawn buggy to a school quite a few miles from where we had settled. I was in second grade at the time; Hazel was in seventh. She drove us through acres and acres of pastureland where great herds of Texas longhorns grazed. It seemed dangerous in ways, but we always managed to arrive safely at school.

As soon as possible, our dad and a few other settlers built a one-room schoolhouse, also serving as our church, much closer to our dugout home. Here we finished the rest of our grade school education. We walked or rode horses to school, encountering many experiences along the way. We killed rattlesnakes, played with tarantulas, watched prairie dogs dart in and out of their holes, and eyed lizards of all sizes scampering under and around the rocks and tumbleweeds. As I mentioned, Hazel, had become quite the horse rider! I remember her scaring my mother and dad to death when she rode a rather wild stallion loaned to us by one of the ranchers. But she came through unscathed! She was an adventuresome cowgirl, unafraid of nearly anything.

As time went along, Dad built an addition to our dugout. This became the room Hazel and I shared. By present-day standards it would not be considered a very fine place, but to us it could be compared to a luxury condo. I remember one night when we were getting ready for bed that Hazel got out a little Princess Pat make-up kit that she had sent for through the mail. She proceeded to do a beautiful make-up job on her face. I watched admiringly for a while and then asked her why she was fixing up herself so nicely when she was just going to bed. She said, "Oh, maybe I will meet my Prince Charming in my dreams. I want to look real pretty!"

Hazel was always considered a really pretty girl. One time she was voted the prettiest girl of all at the Grange Hall Country Dance put on by the ranchers in that widespread settlers' domain. I was so proud of her. I always thought of myself as the ugly duckling in my family. I was scrawny, had almost red hair, and was covered with freckles.

Even as a young girl, I always seemed to look on the darker side of things. I thought everyone else was so much brighter, had so much more going for themselves than I did. I was easily embarrassed, and was convinced that I could not measure up to any of my friends. But Hazel, "the girl with the rose-tinted glasses," saw the bright side. If anyone criticized another, Hazel would turn it right around with something nice to say about that person. If something sad or discouraging happened, she would try to put an alternative light on it that would make it adventuresome, or even romantic.

24

Some years ago when one of my little grandsons was in second grade, he did a school project on the life and times of the western pioneers. He chose to build a little one-room schoolhouse. He put in miniature desks with benches for the children, a desk for the teacher, complete with red marble as an apple for her. Then, he proceeded to tell his teacher that his grandma had gone to a one-room school when she was a little girl. This sparked some interest, knowing that there was still such a person living. As my husband and I were visiting at that time, Nathan suggested that I could tell his class all about my life as a pioneer. The teacher was gracious enough to invite me to their school. It was a revelation to me to see how interested the children were, evidenced by the many questions they asked me.

Near the end of my sharing, one little girl raised her hand and asked, "Did anyone in your family die out there?" I was almost taken aback at this question. I stalled for a second, then went on to tell them that my oldest sister, my parent's first child, had died on the prairie as an infant. I explained that my parents lived in the country without close neighbors, and without transportation to take their precious little one to a doctor. It was thought that she may have had spinal meningitis, and without help, this baby did not survive. My father made the casket, a wooden box, and they buried her out there all alone. My mother told us later about this sad story of how Little Katie, as Mother always called her, had died. I cannot tell this crushing story without tears coming to my eyes.

The reason I tell of this classroom sharing is that it takes me back to Hazel and her response to the death of a sister neither of us ever knew. Some years ago now when we visited Oklahoma City, Hazel and I were reminiscing about our family background. I brought up the story of Little Katie and how crushing it must have been for our young mother. This was Hazel's response: "Well, Honey, I want to tell you that for years and years there was a little white picket fence around that baby's grave. It was a memorial to those pioneer settlers who lived such hard lives."

No matter what the difficult situation, hard-pressed family problem, any criticism of another, any poorly orchestrated event, or any disappointment in life, Hazel had a way of putting a little white picket fence around them, turning them into "something beautiful." This was my sister, "the girl with the rose-tinted glasses."

Just before Hazel turned seventeen, a young man who worked in the oil field fell in love with her and convinced her to marry him. As her eleven-year old sister, I became very caught up with her excitement in planning the wedding. I had seen some wedding dresses in the Sears catalogue and thought every bride should have a long, white dress. She and my mother, however, thought differently. They saw in the catalogue some material for which they sent. It was an ecru-colored pongee material with a border print. When it arrived, she and Mother sewed her wedding dress. She wore this dress as Wayman whisked her off to Muleshoe, Texas to get married. I cried and cried. She was my best friend.

Hazel's dusty road took her back to Oklahoma. For years she lovingly sent me packages with pretty clothes. She made me feel treasured.

*

"Unexpected Turn"

Many western stories and southern ballads later, another real change took place. After five disheartening years, my sister, Clara, who had been taken from us at fifteen, finally broke the silence. She somehow learned where we lived and wrote a letter to my mother. It was a relief to hear from her and to learn that she was well. She was still with this man, Jack, living under an assumed name, and had three small children. In spite of the fact that such an experience had happened to her, we were anxious to see her. The meeting was with some trepidation. It makes me think of the Old Testament Bible story that tells about two estranged brothers, Jacob and Esau, meeting after all the trouble they had experienced. Strangely, though our family was reunited, we never discussed those silent years. My sister had unwittingly gone off with this man, but after realizing her plight, she lived on with him until his death. She bore him eleven children. As far as we knew, they were never officially married.

It was at their urging that we gave up our life on the unyielding prairie, sold our meager belongings, and made a train trip across country to the state of Washington where Clara, Jack and children lived in the small town of Buckley. Though they had little of this world's good, a new life opened up to me. I was able to go through high school there, the first in my whole family to do so. Imagine the changes! I went from a one-room schoolhouse with a handful of students and one teacher for all grades to a brick school, a teacher for each class, and a classroom for each grade. There were all kinds of sports, debate teams, and elocution (speech) contests. Besides all the normal subjects, there were cooking classes and sewing instructions in the Home Economics course. It was indeed a different world!

*

"Little Joe the Wrangler"

"Little Joe the Wrangler"—that's what we called my younger brother when we lived out on the prairies. We were always good friends—Joe and I. We did everything together: chores, riding horses, working, going to school, playing. When we finally made our big move to Washington, of course he went with us. He finished high school two years after I did and then joined the Navy. He did submarine duty and was stationed in Pearl Harbor when it was bombed by the Japanese in 1941. Some years later after the war ended, I got brave enough to ask him about his experience at that awful time. I remember he stood up from the living room couch and said, "Well, I'll tell you one thing." Then he stopped and just walked the floor. He couldn't say another word. I apologized for asking. It was later I learned that his job after the bombing was to go around in a truck and pick up the dead bodies and the wounded. The dead went to the makeshift morgue; the wounded to the hospital. I cried and cried to think my soft-spoken, cowboy brother had been assigned this pitiable wartime task.

Years later, he and his wife moved from town to a more secluded, wooded area which became the quiet setting for a hobby he developed. It was carving animals from wood. He carved birds, including an eagle, sea animals, and many others. He was an artist, a superb craftsman. A stroke in his senior years ended his woodcarving, but not before he had masterfully carved an owl sitting on a fence post. Following his move to a retirement village and being somewhat impaired, he gave this owl to me as a gift. It had a caption which read:

> *and at night*
> *like the cactus in bloom*
> *there was an owl*
> *on every fence post*

This was indeed reminiscent of our life on the prairie when we were kids. In my mind's eye, I can still see dozens of owls perched on fence posts. It is definitely one of those amazing scenes nature imprints on the memory. The carving sits on the fireplace mantle in my family room, a reminder of my life on the prairie saved safely in my brother's art.

Although Joe could no longer do woodcarving, he

found a creative way to do something for a class of impaired veterans of the Second World War who were in a therapy group with him. With the help of his stenographer wife, he published a weekly paper that included poems, jokes and funny articles. His sense of humor had a way to encourage and help relieve some of the lingering emotional trauma brought on by war. Perhaps it was part of his own therapy as well.

The dusty prairie roads of Oklahoma and Texas had eventually taken me and my siblings, save Hazel, further west. These new locations would have their unique ways of changing the courses of our lives significantly. "Little Joe the Wrangler's" dusty road had led him to the horrors of war, a war that had its sad way of shaping his life. My dusty road led me on a much different kind of path. I continue now to share with you a part of my journey that totally and miraculously transformed my life forever after.

*

Part II: "My Journey With Jesus Begins"

It was in that small town of Buckley, Washington, at the age of sixteen, that I was invited to hear the Gospel preached in a little mission church where special meetings were being held. At first, I was wary of the idea of giving my life to Christ, but I was soon convinced that this would fill the longing in my heart to know the One I could look to as a personal Savior and Lord of my life. How I needed His love. I needed His direction and the confidence of belonging. I found it all in JESUS!

*

"Hitting a Roadblock"

Though my new life with Jesus was all wonderful to me, it did not meet the approval of my family, especially my older brother-in-law, Jack. He had a strange hold over our family. We could not love him, yet we were obliged to live under his roof. I especially had opposition from him, and it finally came to the point of him forbidding me to go to church or to meet with my little band of Christians. I was heartbroken, for I had come to love my new life with Christ and with the other new believers who had become my "brothers and sisters."

For a while, I abided by his demands not to attend church, though it was painful to me. But one time, I weakened; I had dinner with a Christian girlfriend and her family. We reasoned that if we just went to the church prayer meeting from her home, my family would not know the difference. So we went. It was so good to be back sitting on those crude benches and singing the happy songs. I was exulting in being there again, when in stalked Jack. He took me by the arm and ushered me out and back home for a lacing-down for my disobedience. Even this did not dampen my joy in serving Jesus, but I really had to learn to stand on my own without the help of Christian fellowship for a long time.

Then one day a miracle happened! As I was slowly walking home from school in our small town, kicking along a rock as I went and thinking about my plight, this same Jack who had rudely yanked me out of church, appeared from an alleyway. He fell into step with me. Out of the clear blue, he took his pipe out of his mouth and said, "Ruth, I want to tell you I have changed my mind. You can go ahead and go to church anytime you want, and I'll not say anything more." This was as much of a miracle to me as was Peter's deliverance out of chains and the prison! If you remember, Peter then looked up his prayer meeting crowd and reported what God had done. That's what I did, too. I was a happy and grateful girl!

*

"Another Miracle"

At the end of high school, I became aware of a new Bible college that had opened in Seattle. It became a burning desire in my heart to go to this school. However, our economic situation had never improved, and we were in the middle of the Great Depression. My poor dad worked on WPA (Workers' Progress Administration), and my mother often worked in other people's homes as a midwife. My brother worked in a Blister Rust Camp, and I sat with little old ladies who were alone. We also picked berries and cherries to make money for school clothes. There was simply no way for me to have any help in going away to school. But, in the middle of an impossible situation, our dear Lord arranged it for me. Through my pastor at that time, we learned of a woman in Seattle who did not have a family of her own and who wanted to sponsor some young person to go to the Bible school. God let me be the one! She paid my tuition through school; I worked for my room and board.

*

"Just What I Needed"

To me, it was like heaven itself to be in school there with all those Christian young people. I learned so much and made many friends. And, it was here that God brought about the miracle of meeting one Sherman Williams. I could get off on a tangent here and tell you some sidelines and circumstances that were interesting and fun. Suffice it to say, God must have known the kind of man I needed in my life to give me confidence and stability. I also met his family whom I came to love and who eventually became the pattern for our life and home in many ways.

In all my life, clear up to this time, we had lived in such poor conditions. I was totally lacking in the kinds of home training that I wished were mine. Our furniture was always a hodge-podge of things we accumulated as time went along. The same was true of our dishes and eating utensils. Nothing matched. I had quite a complex about my home. I never wanted friends to come to see where I lived. In fact, when I was twenty-one, I broke up with Sherman because I just couldn't bring myself to invite him to my home to meet the many and varied people who lived there. There were seventeen of us in all.

After that matter of insecurity was resolved and we

were actually planning to be married, he was going to buy me an engagement ring. However, he did give me a choice of that or anything I might rather have. And do you know what I chose instead of a ring? I asked for a set of silverware that would all match! I have never been sorry I made that choice. My pattern is "First Love," which is also significant to me. I only wear a simple little wedding band which Sherman put on my finger seventy-four years ago. I have never taken it off. As for Sherman, he never wanted me to get him a ring. Instead, he declared, "Honey, I will always conduct myself in such a way that no one will ever question that I am a married man." Pretty classic, wouldn't you say? And I am thankful to say, "He has always been that kind of man."

During our courtship days, we were never able to be together very much. A few times he was able to make a train trip from Great Falls, Montana where he was a youth pastor and song leader for a church there. When he came to see me in Washington, it was a great and special event. When we had to leave one another, we were so sad and could hardly bear to say goodbye. It was during the war years when so many young men were having to leave their sweethearts and young wives to go into the service. This little song was born at that time, and I sang it to Sherman as he boarded the train to leave:

> *Put me in your pocket, so I'll stay close to you;*
> *No more will I be lonesome, and no more will I be blue.*
> *And at the time of parting, there'll be no sad adieu,*
> *For I'll be in your pocket, and I'll go along with you.*[2]

And wouldn't you know it, we had another love song! It goes like this:

> *Somebody loves you, I want you to know,*
> *Longs to be with you wherever you go.*
> *Somebody loves you, and right from the start*
> *Happiness flew into someone's heart.*
> *Somebody loves you each hour of the day,*
> *When you're around, dear, and when you're away.*
> *Somebody loves you; Sweetheart, can't you see?*
> *That somebody is me.*[3]

*

"Beginnings in Billings"

After Bible College and when we were first married, we moved clear away from family and friends in Western Washington to Billings, Montana, where my husband took his first pastorate. We started it "from scratch," as the old saying goes. That isn't really a very nice way to put it. Actually, we started it with a handful of hardy souls Sherman had rallied to the cause just a few months before we moved there as the very young pastor and his bride.

Sherman carried me over the threshold of our small, upstairs apartment. Most people would not have thought it much to exult over, but I thought it was wonderful. We excitedly fixed it up with wedding gifts and the bare necessities. It was the nicest home I had ever lived in.

The most embarrassing thing was that I didn't know how to cook. What a dilemma for me! Here I was supposed to take care of my fine and handsome, young husband and I didn't know how to feed him. And, he was never one to work around the kitchen either! Fortunately, a few months earlier I had this gnawing fear that such a thing might happen. I had seen a cookbook advertised in a "Good Housekeeping" magazine, and had sent for it. The hardback, washable cover read simply, "America's Cookbook."

I took this life-saving volume as my first homemaking assignment. It became my constant teacher, or "Kitchen Bible," all my married years. Besides recipes and how-to's for hundreds of things I had never learned, it included table settings, flower arrangement, and the subject of hospitality. All this was so interesting and exciting to me.

From my basic cookbook learning, I branched out to some things I observed others do. When we were invited to someone's home for dinner or refreshments, I picked out the things I wanted to duplicate when I had occasion to have someone over to our "ever-so-humble" little apartment. Thus began my treasury of special recipes. These are in a file that holds precious memories of those dear, patient people and their willingness to share their tried and true specialties. I always wrote the name of the person who gave me the recipe on the card. One of these recipe-givers was a Norwegian woman who became a part of our church through joining hands with our Norwegian bachelor. They were about fifteen years older than us, but we became good friends. Bertha had worked as a domestic for a wealthy family before coming our way to get married. She knew how to cook wonderful dishes, and also how to serve dinners in what I thought was "fine style." I learned a lot from her. I still have her recipe for a fruit cup that I thought bore a touch of elegance, served in her crystal cocktail glasses. Another recipe I have used as a favorite among my family members is "Swiss Steak." It was from a simple, country cook who prepared it for us in an atmosphere of love and warmth on our first Thanksgiving away from home. I will never forget it. Just recalling these things inspires me again to help make such memories for others who come to our home for fellowship and sustenance. "On-the-job training" was the way my hostessing and hospitality started to emerge. For me it became a beautiful way to reach out and affect others, helping to make the most of what can go on in a home to help fulfill its overall purpose.

Besides beginning our life as a newly married couple in Billings, and besides starting a new church family, we also started our own family. We were blessed to have our little Sharon and Sherman III. Home was taking on a whole new look and feel!

"Another Beginning"

After our first pastorate, we moved with our two small children to Spokane, Washington, where we started another church. Here we enlarged our church and radio ministry, and entered another phase of our lives. This was during the war years and it was difficult to find housing where children were allowed. Eventually, we were able to move into a small apartment in the basement of the new church building we erected during those lean years. Living in the church basement was not the most private situation, but we learned to adapt. Sometimes folks would come to church meetings early to spend a little time visiting with us, but it would frequently be right when I was scrambling to finish dinner clean-up or trying to feed the babies and wished I could be alone. Sometimes they would come for counseling just when my young children needed to be put to bed in a comforting way. At times, I remember finding it necessary to carefully explain to Sharon that she might hear us speaking in private conversation and that she must not tell or talk about anything. I explained that there are times when people are in real need and we wanted to help them know how to pray and look to God for His special help in their lives. As she grew up, she seemed to understand these things. She would pray herself for some of these people and their problems. As it has turned out through all the years, she has been a person who has great empathy for people. She has been used greatly in ministering to the needs of others. Some might think those early experiences would put too much of a burden on a small child, but God knew about it all. He allowed her to grow up to be one of His special servants.

Our church apartment was very small and certainly

had no dining room. It had only a kitchen table. However, we got a fold-up kind of dining table that became a small library table when not in use for company meals. We used it at times for as many as twelve people when we needed to feed more for a company setting. In those situations, we used what we had and did it up as nicely as possible. We knew what it was like to improvise to suit the need. After several years, the church built us a lovely new parsonage. It was wonderful! It gave us more flexibility as we reached out to others.

During this period, I learned much about being a hostess both in the church and in the home through a friend I met in Bible College. She was from a wealthy home, had much experience in social graces, and had graduated from the University of Washington in Home Economics. She became quite a model for me. She was humble, sweet, gracious, and very capable. I loved her. She had a great impact on my life in this area of need. She would often invite a group of young people from the church, along with a few service men, to their home for Sunday dinner. What enjoyable times they were for all of us! It inspired me to want to be able to do those things. It showed me how we might be able to have a ministry to others that reaches out and encompasses more of the things that really count. It was becoming clear to me that despite my itinerant home upbringing and all the insecurities I seemed to have, God was preparing me, as only He could, for a ministry where "home and hospitality" would have an increasing place in my life.

Part III:
"The Warmth of Hospitality… Around Mealtimes"

Telling you stories of "where ah come from" and my early days as a bride and mother is like showing you that I am the "least likely" person to give advice or instructions in homemaking. I am the "least likely" to think I could use the home as an instrument of blessing and outreach to others. But God has helped me to change my prairie chicken mentality into that of a soaring eagle, rising above my self-imposed limitations.

Something Christian author, Ted Engstrom, said has given me a push to stop my "thrashing of wings and flurry of feathers" and make a definite try at a valuable ministry in home and hospitality. He mentioned several Bible characters who were less than the "most likely" in every part of their lives, and yet God used them in significant ways. He writes: "Each of these Bible characters was unique. So are you. Develop your own style. No one has had the same experiences you have had; no one has the contributions to make that you can make. So it's not a question of being better than someone else. Excellence demands that you be better than yourself."[4]

As I have mentioned before, the purpose of this book is to wholeheartedly improve the image of the Christian home. The home, once such a beautiful word that it inspired songs, poems and connotations of love, warmth and security, has become almost an institution of dying embers. Can the flame be rekindled? Can we set some "home fires burning" again? There is a need to encourage young couples to tend their fires with care, love and diligence. So many wonderful things can be bred, fostered and developed in the home environment to influence relationships and ministry to others. So many families today are broken, divided and fractured—"dysfunctional" is the word now being used. There are singles, single parents and other kinds of relationships. We who have traditional homes and families are almost intimidated about voicing ways and means to improve "home fires" across our land. Too often, young people are not made aware of biblical principles regarding marriage, faithfulness, and the consequences of violating vows. They need to be reminded of the rewards of living according to God's standards. It is important to extol the worth and values of trusting God's Word as to what is expected, proper, and what will bring great blessing and true happiness.

In our day, we must begin to recover a sense of devotion or heartfelt zeal for the home. It must be viewed as a wholesome and desirable place that commands our presence, our conscious efforts, and a created atmosphere of love and acceptance for all who reside there.

Now, many, many years after my humble beginnings, I have become a veteran homemaker-wife, mother, grandmother and great grandmother. In 1990, my husband and I celebrated our Golden Wedding Anniversary. It was a glorious event! Memories from so many years were revived in the love story, songs, and the declaration by all of our children and grandchildren through the lyrics of the finale song, "As for me and my house, we will serve the Lord." By the year 2008, when my husband passed away, we had celebrated nearly sixty-eight years together. It was a miracle of God's grace!!

*

"Making Home a Priority"

Reading through the Bible each year, I have underlined any verse, phrase or idea that has impressed me. One day, going through the events in David's life, I read about the exciting occasion when God allowed him and the appointed people—the musicians, the singers, and indeed all His chosen people—to bring the awesome Ark of God to the prepared place for it in Jerusalem. There was great celebration. David blessed the people in the name of the Lord, and then, interestingly enough, he gave them gifts. It says he gave a loaf of bread, a cake of dates, and a cake of raisins to each Israelite man and woman. Then comes this special line as written in I Chronicles 16:43: "Then all the people left, each for their own home, and David returned to bless his family." I am glad he did that. That is what I want to do: bless my family. That's where it all must begin. After all my service among others, public worship and praise to God, I want to return home and bless my family. "If it is possible, as far as it depends on you, live at peace with everyone." (Romans 12:18) I want to be affirming, loving, deferring to others. The atmosphere of the home should say: "I love you. I'm glad you are here!"

In the first three chapters of the Book of Nehemiah, we read of the rebuilding of the broken down walls of Jerusalem. The leaders and their families were assigned a section of the wall closest to their house for which they would be responsible. They put the gates with bolts and bars in place for the protection of their loved city and their homes. We, too, must use such care for the protection of our precious families. I was impressed with the diligence of one family that had only daughters. The girls pitched in and worked until their part of the wall was finished. Hooray for the gals! (Nehemiah 3:12) They did their part. We must do our part!

In this day, it seems the home has been reduced to a place for individuals to rush in and rush out, without a chance to talk to or relate to one another in any meaningful way. Television is the dominant sound. Are other things more powerful than God's ways and principles? Is Satan winning over the nuclear family? It seems that way. Let us who believe in God's ways of righteousness rise to the challenge, and in forthright determination allow our homes to become a creative workshop of effective ideas for loving and serving God. Let us develop family members who ascribe to true values, real love, and active concern for each other. Then, we should care for others, as we ourselves are enlarged to minister to all whose lives we touch.

Awhile back, I read in an article something like this: "A child is like a seed. You water and care for it the best you know how. And then it surprises you and grows all by itself into a beautiful flower!" That's the way I feel about my three daughters. They have grown into beautiful flowers, useful handmaidens for the Lord. And our pastor son has grown into a stalwart "tree planted by the rivers of water," offering advice and shelter to many whose lives he has touched with his shepherd heart. Their mates and their children form great teams of love, affection, and protection for their homes. "I have no greater joy than to hear that my children are walking in the truth."

(III John 1:4)

*

"Hospitality: Jesus as Host"

Have you ever thought of Jesus as a host for any kind of gathering? Or, have you ever thought of Him as being a guest and wondered how He conducted Himself? I got to thinking about Bible examples where Jesus Himself becomes our model in so many wonderful ways.

Imagine that group of people out there on the Judean hillside who had been listening to His teachings. They numbered more than 5,000! He was so aware of their human needs—even their needs for lunch! The disciples wondered how on earth they could furnish food for so many hungry mouths, but Jesus had a plan. He used what was on hand—barley loaves and small fish from a little boy's lunch.

In His own precious way, He multiplied that boy's lunch to meet the need of all who were there. Just think how that boy must have felt to know God used his lunch for such a huge undertaking! Jesus organized this whole event. The people were to sit down on the grass in groups of fifties and hundreds. The twelve disciples served, and then Jesus gave thanks and blessed the food. The people ate as much as they needed. Then the clean-up crew took over! They put all the leftovers in baskets so nothing was wasted. Jesus, as host on that occasion, had it all under control. That was miraculous in more ways than one. (And don't forget, there were women and children at lunch, too!)

At the memorable Last Supper, in the most traumatic hours before His betrayal, trial and crucifixion, Jesus was still able to act as a host to His men. He made the necessary arrangements through His disciples for all the physical elements of that farewell dinner together: the reserved place, the food, and the guest list. All had arrived when Jesus realized there was no servant to wash their dusty feet. It is awesome to think of the Lord of the Universe kneeling down before these men, girding Himself with a towel, and washing their feet. He did what needed to be done when no one else offered. This is a great example of his humility as host!

"The Servant's Heart"

In the pride of misguided busyness,

  a brother's need becomes only a quick prayer,

But HE laid aside His garments.

In the selfish security of doing,

  I can shelter myself from the depths of spiritual care,

But HE took a towel and girded Himself.

In the common place most of all,

  the need often goes unseen,

But HE poured water and washed the disciples' feet.

In the time I have acted,

  my pride of doing shows that in my flesh dwelleth

no good thing,

But HE wiped their feet."[5]

  -Bill Drury

  (one of our church's college-aged men)

Another time, Jesus invited His men to a fish fry on the shore of the Lake of Galilee. He got it all together, then called to them, "Breakfast is ready; come and get it!" I believe they were rather dumbfounded at this show of His willingness to meet their need at a rather discouraging time. I imagine it was the most delicious breakfast they had ever had. After serving them, they had a good talk together. Notice how Jesus took the natural opportunity of breakfast to teach and inspire them to further devotion, love and commitment to follow Him.

*

"Hospitality: Jesus as Guest"

Besides being a gracious host, we find Jesus as a guest in various social settings. Consider the following examples we discover in the New Testament.

At age twelve, Jesus went on a trip to Jerusalem with His family, relatives and friends for the Passover Feast. When His traveling group was finally on its way home again, Jesus lagged behind because of other "pressing business." He was found in the Temple visiting with the rabbis. The Gospel of Luke records that Jesus was attentively listening to these leaders and respectfully asking questions. They were astonished at His understanding. I love the line that says, "And Jesus grew in wisdom and stature, and in favor with God and man." (Luke 2:52) This shows His winsome acceptance by others, even at an early age. Though he was not yet at a place in life to "host" these men, He had his own way to engage these learned religious leaders in meaningful conversation and dialogue. He already sensed the Father's call and took hold of these early leadership opportunities as they were presented to Him. He was open to them; He was ready for them; He took advantage of them. (Luke 2:41-52)

As a young man, Jesus was invited to a wedding. He attended and helped redeem an embarrassing moment for the bride's parents by turning water into fresh wine! Though very unexpectedly asked by His mother to do something to help in this social gathering, He was ready at a moment's notice to do all He could to make this occasion a success. His intervention at the wedding was His first public miracle. This important event in the life of a young couple and their families was another opportunity for Him to be available to turn this reception into a happy memory. Weddings—even weddings—were fitting places to show His love as an invited guest.

On another occasion, a Pharisee asked Jesus to dine with him. Jesus astounded His host and the guests by forgiving a sinful woman who interrupted the party as she approached Him, bowing at His feet. He taught this lesson: "'Therefore, I tell you, her many sins have been forgiven—as her great love has shown. But whoever has been forgiven little loves little.'"

(Luke 7:47) Here again, Jesus was available to step in and assist the host as he dealt with an unexpected arrival at the dinner. He had a masterful way of knowing how to handle this unusual encounter at mealtime with a table-full of men.

Still another time, Jesus was invited into the home of an important Pharisee where He was asked some very challenging questions about healing on the Sabbath. After answering them, He took the mealtime occasion to address their eagerness to choose "best seats" by giving them a poignant lesson on humility. (Luke 14:1-5) As a guest, He was ready for interaction, for sharing of ideas, for offering teaching "around the table."

The tax collector, Zacchaeus, also invited Jesus to visit in his home for dinner. Jesus accepted the invitation, but was criticized by others for associating with a rich publican known for swindling money. Jesus countered this critical spirit among the other guests by bringing salvation to this repentant Jew. Another lesson at mealtime! (Luke 19:1-10)

These and other incidents show that wherever Jesus was a guest, He brought help or blessing in some way. He turned mealtimes into memorable occasions. Though some of Jesus' responses to others were miraculous acts that He could do because He was the Son of God, His example prompts us to do many kind and noble things that will border on the miraculous if we allow Him to use us to do His will. This can be as simple as a smile, a reassuring word to a child or older person, helping in an emergency, a gift, a flower, a card, letter or phone call, a plate of cookies, or any deed of kindness.

It is interesting, too, that Jesus took advantage of so many of these guest/host situations to teach some important truths. We, too, can follow His lead by being aware of how we can turn even our mealtimes into teaching/learning experiences as we reach out in hospitality.

All our service and showing of kindness to others has to be done "in the midst of life," not just during convenient, perfect or planned times. That means it may come at busy times, as well as over-the-long-haul...all done "in Jesus' name."

*

"Hospitality Throughout the Bible"

Reading through the Bible each year, I have noticed many examples of hospitality. God considered it important enough to record these in His Word and left them for our information, for our consideration. Note some of these sightings.

At Abram's victory over enemy kings, he was met by Melchizedek, priest of the Most High, who served him bread and wine and blessed him. (Genesis 14:18) I am sure it was a sweet wine!

When three strangers came to Abraham, "He said, 'If I have found favor in your eyes, my lord, do not pass your servant by. Let a little water be brought, and then you may all wash your feet and rest under this tree. Let me get you something to eat, so you can be refreshed and then go on your way--now that you have come to your servant.' 'Very well,' they answered, 'do as you say.'" (Genesis 18:3-5)

He [Laban] said to Abraham's servant who had come seeking a bride for his master's son, "'Come, you who are blessed by the Lord,' he said. 'Why are you standing out here? I have prepared the house and a place for the camels.' So the man went to the house and the camels were unloaded. Straw and fodder were brought for the camels, and water for him and his men to wash their feet. Then food was set before him, but he said, 'I will not eat until I have told you what I have to say.' 'Then tell us,' Laban said." (Genesis 24:31-33)

(In today's vernacular we might say, "We have a place to park your R.V.!")

On the occasion of the angel's announcement to

Manoah that he and his wife would have a son, Samson, this "father-to-be" said to the angel, "'We would like you to stay until we prepare a young goat for you.'" (Judges 13:15)

At the time when young Saul was chosen to be the first king of Israel, Samuel, the prophet, took Saul and his servant into the great hall and placed them at the head of the table, honoring them above the other special guests. (I Samuel 9:22)

In the account of the Shunamite woman and her husband, the Bible records that they built a special room to use for the prophet, Elisha, whenever he passed their way. They furnished it simply and made it available to the man of God. (II Kings 4:8-17)

During the rebuilding of the wall of Jerusalem, Nehemiah pled with the wealthy Jews not to oppress their poor brothers, but to help them recover their possessions. Nehemiah himself modeled great hospitality by regularly feeding 150 Jewish officials at his table, besides visitors from other countries. (Nehemiah 5:17)

In Proverbs 31, Solomon, in describing the qualities of a truly noble wife, includes her desire to reach out in the warmth of hospitality by sewing for the poor and giving generously to the needy.

Lydia, a businesswoman who met the Lord and was baptized through the Apostle Paul's ministry in Thyatira, asked Paul and the other Christians to be her guests: "'If you consider me a believer in the Lord,' she said, 'come and stay at my house.' And she persuaded us." (Acts 16:15b)

Paul says to the Romans, "Share with the Lord's people who are in need. Practice hospitality." (Romans 12:13)

In the Gospel of Luke, we find Martha serving dinner for a group of believers, including Jesus and His disciples. She had let the work so absorb all her attention that she was worried and upset. She lost sight of the purpose of the whole thing—causing others to think of Him! I am sure Jesus spoke to her in a gentle manner when he said, "Martha, Martha... you are worried and upset about many things, but few things are needed—or indeed only one. Mary has chosen what is better, and it will not be taken from her." (Luke 10:41-42)

Here we take note that Jesus wanted Martha to understand the deeper goal of hospitality.

In giving guidelines regarding the care to be offered Christian widows, Paul remarks that a widow eligible for assistance by the church should be one "...well known for her good deeds, such as bringing up children, showing hospitality, washing the feet of the Lord's people, helping those in trouble and devoting herself to all kinds of good deeds." (I Timothy 5:10)

In mentoring Titus, Paul advises a "pastor must be hospitable, one who loves what is good, who is self-controlled, upright, holy and disciplined." (Titus 1:8)

When the Apostle Peter was teaching Christian Jews scattered throughout the world, he counseled them in this way: "Above all, love each other deeply, because love covers over a multitude of sins. Offer hospitality to one another without grumbling. Each of you should use whatever gift you have received to serve others, as faithful stewards of God's grace in its various forms." (I Peter 4:8-10)

These sightings from Old Testament and New Testament are but some of the Bible's examples showing the importance of hospitality. Indeed the various graces of hospitality provide important threads throughout the centuries, threads of God's kindness to be extended freely and generously to others.

*

"Seasons of Hospitality"

As we consider some of the practical aspects of sharing hospitality, it is important to keep in mind that various seasons of our family life, as well as the circumstances of each season, influence the type of hospitality we will be able to offer. What we are able to do when we are young marrieds is quite different than what we can do as children arrive, grow up and eventually leave our home. Our financial abilities, work schedules, house size, and even geographic location have definite influences on how we do hospitality. Perhaps some personal experiences will help clarify.

In our first pastorate, we had a small, two-room, upstairs apartment with only the bare necessities. We had no financial backing from a "mother" church or denomination. We had to do it on our own. But thank God, we didn't have to do it all alone! Our dear Lord was our great and loving helper. He provided for us in ways that I think are comparable to the way Elijah was fed by the ravens. When a bag or box of groceries was left at our little abode, we accepted it as a gift left by an angel. What a wonderful memory.

Though God always seemed to provide in some rather miraculous ways, I must admit that I often felt there was so little we could do in entertaining others. We barely had enough for ourselves. Besides, I didn't know how to cook. What a dilemma! I learned a lot from observing other dear women in our small church who always seemed eager to help me. Little by little, I learned to copy these examples and became a growing learner and "Queen of the Kitchen," as some called me in later years. (Of course, now I am a seasoned old cook—and don't mind the title!)

I will never forget a time early in our first pastorate when a couple with a large family shared with us their homespun hospitality. What a gift it was to receive an invitation to join them for our first Thanksgiving meal away from home. Though living in rather simple circumstances, they warmly included us in their circle for the holiday season. The hostess, a country cook, served us delicious Swiss Steak, along with a full course of tasty home-grown food. I copied down her Swiss Steak recipe and it has become my family's favorite meat entrée for many special occasions. She never knew how often I would copy her great dinner menu for many years to come. I had learned from an experienced homemaker another grace of warm-hearted hospitality, the kind that makes room for those without family close by to share a holiday dinnertime.

Another creative and loving gesture of hospitality was extended to us during a totally different season of life when we were on a trip through the southern United States. The traveling team of six included two teenage daughters, our oldest daughter and her husband, and my husband and me. Our daughter and husband, who were missionaries in Quito, Ecuador for many years, especially wanted to touch base with some fellow missionaries who were on a home ministry assignment in Florida. Two hours before we were to arrive in their city, we phoned to ask if it would be okay to stop by for a short visit. The man was graciously anxious for us all to come by, even though his wife was out of town. He and his teenage daughter quickly found a way to accommodate spur-of-the-moment guests. They ordered a Kentucky Fried Chicken dinner for us all. However, they didn't serve it in the usual cardboard containers. They nicely arranged the chicken on a big platter, the coleslaw in a glass serving bowl, and the biscuits on a tray covered with a white napkin. They made this take-out style dinner into a delicious banquet. We enjoyed a lovely visit as a result of their "short-notice" hospitality. I think Jesus was pleased with their kindness to us wayfaring travelers. They had chosen to share a meal with us under awkward, last-minute circumstances. But, they adapted, were flexible, and creative—all at the same time!

A plan that my husband and I adopted as the years went on was to choose a couple who had shown us a kind favor and provide a "thank-you" dinner for them. We not only invited them, but asked them to invite three or four couples of their choosing to join us. In this way, we got to make friends with people we would not have had occasion to know more than by just a handshake and "good morning" at church. After the camaraderie at the dinner table, they were invited into the living room where we shared a bit of our life stories—how they came to know Christ and how they came to our church. Sometimes we sang a song that meant a lot to them, or they shared a Scripture that had changed their lives. What engaging stories we have heard about transformed lives because of Jesus!

Sometimes the thought of inviting and organizing an evening of hospitality is a bit overwhelming. Why not "share the load" rather than have the pressure of doing it all on your own. Try this! Put together a small group of friends. Each one takes a turn having a potluck dinner in his/her home. The host prepares the main hot dish and the others bring the rest of the dinner. Some have small homes and may be hesitant to invite guests, but they should be encouraged to handle it any way they can arrange it. For example, you could serve on trays or outdoors so as to make it more feasible for all to become acquainted, begin to understand each other, and start forming good friendships. Tailor your hospitality to ways with which you feel comfortable, with ways that reflect you. You may know other people who have delightful ideas from which you can benefit, ideas where planning is less intensive, simpler, more casual. Make hospitality a joy, not a burden; a ministry, not an obligation.

On another occasion, in another season of life, we invited my grandson, his wife and four children for Sunday dinner. They were back in the United States from Lima, Peru, where they were missionaries. As we sat around the dining table and started to enjoy our old-fashioned roast dinner, their eleven year-old son announced, "Grandma, you are an awesome cook!!" Imagine how that pleased me! Everybody had a good laugh at his spontaneous declaration.

I have come a long way in developing and honing the grace of hospitality since our early, newly married days in Billings, Montana. The important thing? Just get started. Take it step-by-step. You'll be amazed at how your willingness to do as you can, when you can, with what you have, can be a blessing and encouragement to others. To give hospitality is a joy; to receive hospitality is a treasured gift.

"Hospitality's Forgotten People"

As a result of being in pastoral work for so long, I noticed that there are some groups of people that are often forgotten when it comes to being invited into other people's homes. I knew I needed and wanted to address this oversight which included singles (both men and women, young and old), divorced, never married, widowed, and families with children. After some thought, I felt the Lord gave me some innovative ways to include these often forgotten folk. In fact, this idea came to me in response to a message I had heard about the importance of the family of believers acting "as a family."

I decided to invite a table full of such dear church friends. First, I wanted our pastor and his wife to be there. Next, I invited a family consisting of a mother, father, with grade school and high school daughters. I also invited three single men—one a school teacher, one our new church music director, and the other, a funeral director who had recently taken such loving care of my dear husband's memorial service arrangements. Also, there were two younger divorced women, one couple who had recently joined our church, as well as one college-aged girl. Hardly any of these people knew each other personally. As we enjoyed dinner and conversation together, I tried to encourage them to think of each other as brothers and sisters in our church family. They all seemed to really enjoy the occasion. I hope the experience made them feel like an important part of the family of God.

Sometimes our invitations to dinner have included couples that have several children. I ask the couple if they would like their family to come, or if they would rather come with several other couples. On one occasion, a couple responded that they would love to come as a family in order for their kids to learn how to function in a company setting—sort of a "Good Manners at the Table" lesson. So, that is what we did! As families with children are seldom invited to other people's homes, this was an opportunity for these parents to help train their children as well as an opportunity for us to become acquainted with their children. On the other hand, some couples found it special to socialize with adult friends. Being without their children for an evening gave them a break from their on-the-job parenting and allowed them time and leisure for adult conversation. No matter which option was taken, either provided valuable time with younger couples or families.

Having singles, widows, new people, or those experiencing sorrow over for dinner is definitely a way to show your interest in these often "forgotten" people. If having them over for a meal is not conducive to your schedule, taking any of these people out for coffee or dessert is another possibility. No matter the situation or family status, just being willing to invite others in or offering to take them out is a step in extending the warmth of hospitality.

*

"Sweet Sixteen-ers"

As I came into my senior years, I recognized another way to share hospitality with some of the other seniors in our church. I found out that a number of other women were born the same year that I was—1916! I decided to form a little band of women called "The Sweet Sixteen-ers." I invited them to join me for dinner in my home. We all brought "Sweet Sixteen" birthday cards for one another and a picture of ourselves at sixteen. We each told about what was happening during our high school days at the time the photo was taken. One dear woman recounted how she had a baby out of wedlock and desperately had to find work to support herself and her little infant girl. This was during the Great Depression at the time of World War II. Times were difficult and her circumstance added to the struggles. Sharing this with us made us feel closer to her and gave us a deeper understanding of this sister.

All the gals told their own stories and shared their interests and school memories.

Each year following this initial dinner together, we had another "Sweet Sixteen" birthday party. One time we made it a Hawaiian luau and dressed in muumuus and leis. Any who had husbands brought them along for the occasion. These were indeed fun times! This variation of hospitality encompassed older people, people with stories and memories that needed to be shared. It provided a way to keep our bonds of friendship sweet over many years as God threaded our lives together in a tapestry of devotion, color and delight.

*

"Some 'Basics' for Hospitality"

In all aspects of serving, remembering a few basic things can help us be ready for guests and put our minds at rest. Consider the suggestions in this checklist:

- Tidy house. Try to do as much cleaning the day before the guests are coming.
- Table readiness. In preparing for more formal dinners, try doing the following the day before if possible: plan and put together the centerpiece and table setting; clean and polish the silverware unless you are fortunate to

have the beautiful stainless steel sets available.

- Preparation of food—shop ahead! In order to do this you must:

  a. List your invited guests—how many?

  b. Make out the complete menu.

  c. List the things you need under each menu item to ensure you have at hand all the ingredients for your meal.

- On the day of the meal there will be lots to do!

  a. First thing in the morning, bake or prepare any special dessert, as well as anything that needs to be chilled or frozen.

  b. Vegetables—Prepare any that you can keep in cold water until it is time to cook them. Determine when you actually need to start cooking them.

  c. Gauge the time you need to start the meat.

  d. Consider how long it takes to put together the salad or warm rolls.

- Your own appearance. An experience I had taught me a lesson about being a prepared hostess. One time we invited a good-sized family, new to our church, to our home for dinner. All day I busily went about the preparation I thought was necessary. Too soon it was time for the guests to arrive! The doorbell rang and I was caught in my steamy work clothes! I was so embarrassed and ashamed. I quickly vanished to my room to change while my dear husband entertained the friends until I appeared again refreshed and ready to serve our dinner. I never let that happen to me again! From then on, I made it a habit to get myself ready for company at least an hour before they were due to arrive at my "welcome sign."

*

"Blessings of Hospitality"

The decision to use hospitality as a ministry of opening our hearts and homes to others carried with it a host of blessings, blessings never expected. The Lord definitely has a way of surprising us with His own version of rewards and favors that have their priceless way of encouraging and spurring us on. I share here with you some of those blessings spread out over the years and seasons of family life. Keeping in mind "where 'ah come from," perhaps you will see how God tailor-made these blessings for me. How I praise Him for being such a personal God.

It was when we left our church in Spokane, Washington

where we pastored for ten years, that one of these outstanding blessings of encouragement arrived. The blessing came in a very specially chosen farewell gift. It was a whole set of beautiful Bavarian china, three sizes of stemware, service for twelve! Little did they realize that this gift of lovely, matching dinnerware was just another way God was showing me His love and preparing me for further service ahead. This gift has since been used to serve hundreds and hundreds of guests. The dishes were God's way to multiply our ministry of hospitality.

Years of family life passed bringing us to the conclusion of another twenty-year pastorate in Castro Valley, California. Soon after we resigned, the church had a beautiful Appreciation Day for us including farewell gifts—a new car for my husband and a dining room set for me! Why was the dining room set so totally special to me? In the first place, it was such an incredible surprise. I was not hankering for or planning to get a different set from the one we had used for all the years we had lived in Castro Valley. It had straight, simple lines and a laminated top. It was used every day for every meal. Some of the chairs had become less than sturdy because of my giant-sized sons-in-law, but I always thought the set was practical and good enough. But, when I saw the gorgeous fruitwood dining table, the high-backed, impressive chairs, and the imposing matching hutch all shown off with the huge cellophane bow with my name on it, there were no words to describe how wonderful it was to me! Even more than that, it was an unexpected confirmation of a spiritual experience I had during the year prior. I had sought the Lord to help me determine what He wanted me to focus on in service for Him at this approaching stage in my life. One day, He impressed on me through His Word the grace of hospitality. Though our home had always been opened to others all throughout our pastorates, He seemed to be emphasizing that this grace, this gift, could be even more greatly used.

Very soon after my commitment to pursue this challenge from the Lord, He opened up an opportunity for us to have just as many of our church family as could come to a series of fellowship evenings in our home. As a result, for a whole month, five nights each week, we had groups of 35-45 people in our home. It was a special month indeed. I loved it! So, it seemed God really took me at my word. It was all a blessing. Seeing the dining room set on that Farewell Day at our church, it was as if the Lord was saying, "Here, Ruth, are some more tools to work with. Take them and use them for Me." So, that's what we did. In fact, we had to build a house around that set of furniture! Oh, and did I mention how nice it was that it all matched? Once again, God had chosen to bless the ministry of ongoing hospitality. His encouragement was timely, perfect, just what I needed to inspire me even as my senior years were beginning to set in. You see, all along our dear Lord was taking the "little lunch" of my life, as ignominious as it has been, and was using it!

Another blessing of hospitality was the effect that a home open to others had on our children. Because our home was a place of comings and goings for all kinds of people in many different settings, our children became exposed to the natural ways of showing God's love and care for people through mealtimes and meaningful conversation. They learned the graces (even from childhood) of welcoming people into their lives. Each of our four children gave their hearts to Jesus at an early age and dearly love the Lord Jesus as I do. They are His committed, loyal followers. I have come to increasingly see how He has blessed the lunch of my life through them in a whole variety of ways. They have touched the lives of people for Jesus' sake through pastoring, teaching, music, worship, business, counseling, foreign and home missions, and Christian leadership.

Needless to say, the blessing of hospitality was not only a one-way street. Our guests were often used by God to bless us and inspire our children in His ways. And, besides God's direct blessing in our own children's lives, He multiplied our hospitality through many whom we touched in pastoral ministry. I would like to declare with my friend Jacob of old: "I am unworthy of all the kindness and faithfulness you have shown your servant. I had only my staff when I crossed this Jordan, but now I have become two camps." (Genesis 32:10)

Part IV:
"The Warmth of Home... Besides Mealtimes!"

Stirring up the embers to keep "home fires burning" includes more than opening your home in hospitality to others through meals, that wonderful ministry to one another "around the table." Development of a warm and inviting atmosphere called "home" also means encouraging children to explore and tend to talents and gifts that will contribute to their own maturity, enjoyment, and nurture practical ways to serve God with their lives. It also means facing some of the very real heartaches and challenges that surface in any family. It means learning how to develop family traditions that are meaningful and which will become some of the special glue that binds family in unique and signature ways. And...there is no question that any talk of the Christian home would be incomplete without speaking to the attention that a healthy, loving marriage needs as a solid foundation for the Christian family. Thus, the next section of these writings will speak to "the happy sounds of music," the "sad sounds of heartache," the "celebration sounds of Christmas traditions," and the "rewarding sounds of love." Though they are based on my own family's experiences, perhaps they will serve as examples of these additional and very important ingredients needed in "keeping the home fires burning."

May the Lord use His work in these several areas from my life and home to spur you further on, to keep you moving forward, and to give you added joy and hope.

*

"The Happy Sounds of Music"

During our family-rearing years, from the time our first child was six years old until all were away to college, one would constantly hear the sound of music emanating from the "House of Williams."

As I was taking a morning walk through our neighborhood several years ago, many sweet memories of an earlier season of family life came flooding back to me. Passing a certain house at approximately the same time each morning, I would hear the sound of music. A budding pianist played scales and simple pieces that I used to hear regularly when our daughters and son took music lessons. I was so pleased to hear these recognizable pieces that I was tempted to stop at this stranger's house and encourage the young musician to keep up the good work! I didn't actually do this, but the experience reminded me again of all the practicing that took place in our home. I think I can say without contradiction from our children that I was their greatest cheerleader for their musical pursuits and accomplishments.

Knowing that music was always a wonderfully enjoyable part of our family and church life, numerous mothers have asked me about ways we were able to turn out musicians that were useful in the Lord's work. How did we develop their interest and expertise in music on through adulthood? And so, I thought it might be helpful to include some of these "frequently asked questions" and give some responses from our experience on our home front.

1. Were you and your husband musicians? My husband and I were not trained musicians, although we were always involved in music. Sherman played the trumpet and guitar. As an older child and teenager, I took basic piano lessons for a limited time; then vocal lessons for a while. We both did considerable singing as soloists and in small groups, participating in radio programs in both our Bible College and churches. However, we wanted our children to have a better opportunity than we had. Although many peers in our circumstances felt

they simply could not afford music lessons, we felt it a necessity.

2. When do you think children should start taking lessons? Our children started taking piano at age six. By this time most children know numbers and letters for reading, making it much easier to progress in learning notes, counting rhythm and manipulating their fingers properly.

3. How did you get your kids to practice? In the early months of them taking lessons, I stayed in the teacher's studio during the lesson to be sure I understood the assignments. During their practice times at home, I felt it was very important to sit with them to see that they practiced correctly. Eventually, of course, they practiced on their own. Though the children branched out to other instruments as time went on, the piano gave them the basics of all that would follow.

4. How did you get in all the practice sessions when you had several taking lessons? We found it best to have the children practice at a regular time each day. There was no question whether or not a child would practice! The child did it consistently as a habit. Before long, the child could play little pieces that delighted his/her own ears!

5. How did you choose teachers? Different teachers throughout the years add their unique ways of teaching various elements of what children need to learn. For example, the first teacher of our two older children was a disabled woman who taught from her wheelchair. She was a cheerful Christian who was the favorite piano teacher in our area. She loved her pupils, following them with interest from beginning days through adulthood. Many of her students became church pianists and musicians. From their earliest lessons, she included a simple gospel song in the assignments. She encouraged them to sing the words while playing, and to keep the right tempo for the song. She caused our children to love their music!

6. What do you do when kids give you problems about taking lessons, practicing, or want to quit? To be honest, our son was not the most eager pianist, but he stuck with it until we let him start trumpet lessons. This was more to his liking! Before the trumpet years, however, he woke up a sleepy piano recital audience by playing and singing, "Little Boy Blue, Come Blow Your Horn." He ended the song with Little Boy Blue snoring loudly "under the haystack fast asleep." When his piano days

finally ended, I was pleased when he invited two school buddies to come to our house to practice their horns in our downstairs recreation room! Adding some "fun" inspired these budding musicians to progress in playing their band music.

One of our daughters had a teacher steeped in classical music. She wanted each beginner piece played like the composer would have played it. Though somewhat tedious, this had it its own positive effect in our little girl's overall training. This same teacher had us buy a packet of portraits of great composers with biographical sketches. Each week, our daughter was to set up one of the portraits in her room. Each morning she was to say, "Good morning, Wolfgang Amadeus Mozart!" This was continued through twenty great classical composers. Their biographical sketches were revered and informative. What a great education she received from those gifted men!

During our oldest daughter's music education, she experienced several kinds of violin teachers. Her first teacher from public school felt Sharon should have private lessons. She directed us to a violin teacher whose European-style approach had a lasting impact on her life.

The teacher's home studio was like a museum of ancient musical instruments. Because she and her husband were German Jewish refugees, they had been part of the classical music world not only in Germany, but in Italy and England. They were authentic Old World musicians! One would have thought nothing mattered in the world but classical music. Sharon developed an exalted opinion of this special couple who gave her an appetite for the classics. This interest increased throughout the years.

When our family moved to Wheaton, Illinois, we looked for a teacher for Sharon. The first one we tried did not seem to be a good fit during this transitional time, so she took a break from lessons that year. Then we were privileged to find a good teacher until she went away to college. Sharon and this woman really bonded. She was a lovely violinist and helped Sharon know how to effectively interpret music. Sharon had also become an accomplished pianist and accompanied her teacher for her own musical appearances. Because they were both violinists, they were complements to each other. That was another growing experience in our daughter's training.

I will now mention our youngest daughter, Merilee. She did not fall into the groove as easily as the others! She learned the piano basics and then was insistent on learning to play the organ. Her real challenge in music, however, came many, many years later as an adult and as a pastor's wife. In the church which they started and pastored, she became the pianist and music leader for their services and worship team. Being thrust into that position, she was dedicated to help the whole of their church ministry and has effectively used the musical training she had received. The early struggles were worth it! (She would agree to that!)

7. Any other tips for inspiring children in music? To encourage our children in their music pursuits, we gave little rewards for playing a piece without making mistakes. When they were beginners, this was colored stickers or stars. This helped teach them not to rush through their pieces, but do them with excellence.

   One time, I heard a music instructor say it would be well not to use the word "practice" but simply say, "Let's play the piano now." Always "playing." That takes it out of the connotation of drudgery.

   Another axiom I heard was: "The most important time of practice is the last fifteen minutes."

   Unless we were away on vacation, we kept the music

going! With more free time when children are not in school, this became a natural time to keep making progress when their lives were not so busy with schoolwork.

We also encouraged singing in vocal ensembles, going to music camps, being in competitions, and playing in bands or orchestras—the joy of playing or singing with others.

The whole intent of giving our children a music education was to make them usable in Christian service. That is what has taken place in the lives of each of them. Count on it! Every Sunday, and many other times in special programs, musicals, and concerts, they are right there performing "in the name of the Lord." Grandchildren and great grandchildren are learning how to pass along the "torch" of music in their generation. Praise God!

Years and years after the children were gone from our home, other ways to keep encouraging the ministry of music were still found! Enclosed here is a letter written to Sharon, our oldest daughter, when she was about twenty-five. Music has a way of following us, of making our hearts sing, and is one of God's favorite ways, or so it seems, to offer Him praise.

TO SHARON, WITH LOVE,

Can you believe it? I'm on my way to Ecuador. Yes, I am Redwood Chapel's newest missionary. Who would have thought a dozen years ago that I would land on a foreign mission field? Not I, and not the Williams Family, and surely not you! But I have had a lot of preparation for "the field" in the years past. This made me ready and waiting for my assignment. In just a few days' time, Pastor (your dad!) and some helpers hauled me into a truck, rushed me over to the Home of Peace, and had me crated for shipment on a boat straight for Quito.

The Williams Family was sentimental and emotional, as you might imagine, saying farewell to another member of their family and home. But priorities had to be put in the right place, and they decided I was the one to go.

To tell the truth, I am thrilled to the highest scale to be on my way, for I know what a useful place I am going to fill in the Erickson home in South America. I am certain I will bring much personal joy to your heart, for your whole life has been so wrapped up in music. Besides that, I will become the basic instrument for music training for Danny, Jens and Amy. I will be predominant in much of your music ministry, "Heralding Christ Jesus' Blessings (HCJB)."

They tell me that missionaries of my kind are hard to come by in Ecuador. They have to be imported from other countries. So, I consider it a key privilege to get to go.

I can hardly wait until Big Marty unpacks me and my belongings and settles me in your home to fulfill my mission in "the regions beyond."

Pray for my safe arrival!

"CONNIE KIM"

(Console Kimball, the Williams' family piano)

*

"The Sad Sounds of Heartache"
Letter to Our Tiny Tim...

****

Dearest Little Tim,

It may surprise you that I would want to communicate with you even though we have not been on the same wavelength for a long time. You see, it was this way—I carried you for nine months. Then you came into this world. I was so sorry you did not stay long on this earth, but God must have had another plan for your life. As your mother, I did not get to see you but one time; that was when they wheeled you into my hospital room. Even then, I wasn't allowed to take you out of the incubator. When my dear husband came in, he said, "Honey, I don't think we're going to be able to take him home with us." What a shock! Such a possibility had never entered my mind. You, my baby boy, would never be able to live on earth in our little family.

I never got to hold you in my arms, nor hold you close to my breast. I could not touch your soft, baby skin or stroke your little arms or kiss you over and over. I did not see you grow to be a toddler, or be in cute pictures playing with Sharon and Sherman, or go off to school, play the piano, participate in sports, have a career, or get married. No, this would have been for your earthly life; yours was to be a home in heaven, whatever it is God designs for such little ones in eternity.

I could not think why such a thing would happen to us. It seemed, as far as we could see, that there was no reason to have such a severe lesson of discipline in our lives. We were a young couple dedicated to the Lord's work. We were training our two children in the ways of the Lord. We followed the Scripture that advises us, "Start children off on the way they should go, and even when they are old they will not turn from it." (Proverbs 22:6) We had been diligent in training our first little girl and boy in all the ways we could think of to put them on the path of walking with Jesus. We taught them many individual Bible verses, longer portions such as The 23rd Psalm and The Lord's Prayer, and many children's songs and choruses. We thought we were doing our part as best we knew.

Timmy, when we lost you, we were dumbfounded, but we went on to make all the arrangements for your demise from our family and earthly life. I picked out the cutest little outfit that had been given to me at the wonderful church baby shower to have you dressed in. I included the prettiest, comfy blanket to put over you when you were placed in the all-white, very small casket. One man carried it out to the cemetery gravesite in Spokane, Washington. It is a beautiful spot in a row of simple, little gravestones all marked as baby resting places. Yours reads, "Baby Boy Williams." If you had lived in our family, your name would have been Timothy Jon Williams. Who knows the why of all this? Only God. He must have had His purpose in it all.

The private graveside service was attended only by family members who were living in Spokane at that time: your dad and me, your older sister and brother, Sharon and Sherman, your dad's sister and husband, and your dad's parents, Mother and Dad Williams. It seems to me that I was the saddest of all to just leave you there, but actually, you were in a much brighter place with all the celestial surroundings and your dear Savior, Jesus Christ.

Tucked away in my Lane cedar chest, along with a few other keepsakes, there is a sweet baby book that was given to me at the shower for you. I had thought it might be filled with congratulation cards, a list of the cute gifts for you, and maybe some pictures of you as an infant. But no; it was a place for sympathy cards and the birth and death certificates for you, my baby boy.

After several weeks, when I had passed a stage of being a stoic, I wondered what to do with all the darling little baby things that had been given at the baby shower. We had stored them for some time in the small crib we had borrowed for you. Our apartment in the church basement was so small that there was no room for a regular-sized baby crib. It began to bother me to see your gifts there day after day, keeping me so mindful of our loss of you. An older couple in our church had offered to store the little treasures that had been intended for you at their home until we decided what to do with them. They had a daughter who worked for the American Embassy in Germany. It had been during World War II and many German families were left destitute. She told them of one young minister and his wife who were expecting their first child. They wondered if we might want to send our baby layette to this couple. That is what we did. We added to your clothes some toys and a supply of baby food. This seemed like a fitting closure for saying a truly fond farewell to you and for your things to go to another "PK" (Preacher's Kid). I know you are resting in peace. I loved you so.

Mother love,

RUTH WILLIAMS

*

I must tell you that one of the sweetest lessons I learned from this sad experience is how much we must be aware of the tremendous privilege God allows us in the gifts of those children who arrive safely into our home. Never must we take for granted the opportunity He assigns us to be foundation-builders in their lives.

Two years after the death of little Tim, we were allowed to have a tiny, baby girl who was perfect in every way. Oh, how we loved her. We were so thankful for her and her dainty features. I loved every part of taking care of her, including the nighttimes of being awakened to feed her, as well as caring for her baby needs to be diapered to make her comfortable. The messy little jobs were not even resented. I was so glad to have her there with me to love and cuddle. I gloried in the fact that I had such a privilege. That baby girl, Constance Joy, has always been our constant joy! How we have treasured her life and her place in our family.

Another two years passed and we were given another darling baby girl, Merilee, to bless our home and complete our family. These two little daughters that arrived after the death of Timmy have always been close friends. What a joy this has been to us. Sharon and Sherman, nine and ten years older than Connie and Merilee, were affectionately called "the big kids"; the younger girls were always referred to as "the little kids." Still are! Perhaps it was the loss of Timmy that helped me better appreciate each of our children in all their uniqueness. Needless to say, I love my family!

It was about thirty-seven years after our Timmy went to heaven that we received a phone call from Connie Joy announcing the birth of their first child. "It's a boy!" she exclaimed, "and his name is Timothy." In her sweet way she was carrying on the remembrance of her brother whose life was ever-so-brief. Bless her.

In my need to learn all I could from this "sad sound of heartache" season in our family life, I came up with my own version of personal therapy. This therapy involved keeping a list of some of the things God taught me. I share them with you....

1. It has made me so much more aware of the suffering of other people. Through the years, I've had many opportunities to try to console young parents who have lost a child. Though I have desired to do an even more effective job in this ministry of consolation, I have received some comments from others telling how it has helped them just to know someone else who has gone through such trauma.

2. Also, I have seen how this loss affected our older children, making them much more sensitive to how such family loss affects others. Children learn from us how to accept loss.

3. Soon after this experience of the loss of our baby, a young couple planning to go to the mission field came to speak at our church and tell of their need for financial support. They came to have dinner with us in our small church basement apartment. They had one baby boy. He was really tired and fussy from their long day of traveling. He kept crying and crying. It was embarrassing and perplexing for the young couple to know how to handle the situation. I felt so sorry for the mother. I took her and the baby back to our children's bedroom to see if we could quiet him and put him to bed. I put my arm around her and briefly told her about losing our own baby boy and how I wished he were still with me to care for and comfort when he needed me. I told her not to fret because her baby was upset, but to consider him her God-given treasure, and then ask our dear Lord how to take care of him the best she could. A few weeks later, I received a thank-you note from her, referring to our little talk in the bedroom and how it

helped her be more thankful rather than despair over a tired baby's crying. She went on to confide in me that her husband was bent on going to the mission field, in spite of her reservations about it. She was undergoing a personal struggle that had upset her. She thanked me for talking to her that night. It really wasn't much that I did, but in sharing with her my experience of sadness, it helped to calm her troubled spirit. I have kept the note she sent me as a reminder of how God uses the things we go through to bring hope to others as we are willing to share the testimony of His grace in our own lives.

*

"The Celebration Sounds of Christmas Traditions"

Looking at this old world's system, one finds less and less of Jesus being the focal point of the true Christmas celebration—Christ coming into the world to be the mighty Savior for all mankind. As the world's "slow stain" becomes more obvious in Christmastime observances, Christmas is clearly emerging as a mere holiday. The focus seems to be on a "jolly old man, St. Nicholas," who is able to ride on a flying sleigh driven by his reindeer with their funny names. Just think, even with his huge pack of gifts, Santa can go down the chimney into each home in the world on one designated night so that every good boy and girl receives just what he or she wants. By the next week, however, the prized gift is broken or set aside. Children (and adults!) discover that the gift they couldn't wait to receive wasn't "just what they wanted" after all. What an experience in futility.

Even as a Christian family, we found it challenging to find ways to keep Christ the center of the Christmas celebration. With such a major emphasis on the more reciprocal aspect of traditional gift-giving, we found ourselves unnecessarily sidetracked from the true joy of "giving in Jesus' name." How could we shift the emphasis back to the Gift of Christmas— Jesus? As parents of children in our home, as well as when we became grandparents, we remained on search to discover some traditions that in very practical ways might turn our true attention to Jesus.

One thing we learned as the years have come and gone, is that we couldn't celebrate in the same way at every stage of family life. We had to adapt to the growing stages of development and understanding of our children, grandchildren, and great grandchildren.

The changing nature of any family, whether in size,

contour or marital relationship, contributes to the traditions or creative ideas that can most effectively point our celebrations toward Jesus. I share with you a series of ideas or experiences we have had that may be of help to you as you tailor-make your family celebration. Perhaps they will at least serve as a starting point to spur you on to your own unique ways to bring Jesus to the forefront of your family at Christmastime.

*

1. Because Christmas is Jesus' "birthday," having a special dinner for the "Unseen Guest of Honor" has always seemed most appropriate. A specially decorated table (or tables), our favorite foods (often brought by various families included in the celebration), plus a birthday cake for Jesus helped create a festive atmosphere. The cake (decorated with miniature nativity pieces) was brought out with ceremony and candles burning. "Happy Birthday" was sung to dear Jesus with great gusto and clapping. And then, what can be done for the "rest of the party?"

2. One of the most basic things you can do in your goal to keep Christ the focal point is to set aside a special time on Christmas Eve or Christmas Day to read aloud the Christmas Story from the Bible. Choose a translation

that you think will be most understandable to even the youngest in your family circle. It may be more beneficial to read the account from a children's storybook. Choose a family member (or more) who will read with expression, allowing the story to be captured with its sense of wonder. Pictures? Show them! For your story time, create an atmosphere—fireside, by the tree, dimly lit, or whatever makes it different than the usual.

3. Because children love to be involved and enjoy the hands-on aspect of any gathering, try placing the pieces of a nativity set at various spots around the room. As the story is read, have them find the piece being referred to and bring it to the stable. We have had angels swing down on nearly invisible lines and camels travel from far off in an adjacent room! Make it fun for them. Allow them to "experience" the story with some hands-on expressions.

4. You may also want to use a hymnal to sing the stories of Christmas. Or, you might prefer to just read the lyrics of familiar carols. This, too, can bring a fresh reminder of the wonder of it all.

5. Particularly during certain seasons of our family's life, we agreed that each family unit would offer a "family

presentation" in honor of Jesus. This was an activity or offering that was designed to glorify God and would allow each person, youngest to oldest, to contribute to the festivities. Examples of such presentations that our families have done follow...

a. One family demonstrated how they used Advent candles during the weeks before Christmas to help prepare their hearts for the birthday of Jesus.

b. Another time, a family used squash (yes, the vegetable!) to make puppets to dramatize the Christmas Story.

c. An abbreviated Christmas musical was performed by one family, including both drama, music, and narration.

d. Two teenage cousins decided to do their own very unique presentation. They became their own on-location television crew! One was the cameraman; the other the reporter. They took their gear and went to a popular shopping mall where they recorded people answering this question: "What does Christmas mean to you?" The boys gathered these interviews and presented them at our Christmas celebration. It was so much fun...and informative as well.

e. Another year, the extended family donned costumes that represented the figures and people usually associated with the birth of Jesus. We had Mary, Joseph, the newborn baby, shepherds and shepherd boys, the innkeeper, and children posing as sheep and camels. Men in the family represented the wise men with their gifts for the King of Kings. One young granddaughter standing above our living manger scene made the picture complete. She was wearing a large headpiece made with a star-shaped balloon!

f. One family, clever at writing poetry and stories, took turns reading their unique insights about Christ's birth.

g. Still another year, my husband and I donned mid-Eastern attire and became TV anchors behind a large picture frame! We reported the breaking news about strange things that had happened a fortnight ago. "We've been informed that a baby was born to a peasant girl; unusual circumstances surrounded the birth that are said to be prophetic. This child may be the Messiah that we Jews have been waiting for throughout the centuries. We will be giving more details as they come in."

h. Some read or told classic stories such as "The Little Match Girl." Dressed in costume, one family member read a fictional monologue she had written from the viewpoint of a girl who had accompanied the caravan of wise men.

i. Attired in a long, black dress, I once presented a Christmas monologue called "I Shall Behold Him." It is a fictional story about a young shepherd boy who didn't get to see the Baby Jesus in Bethlehem because he was assigned to stay and guard the flocks while his father and the other shepherds rushed to town to check out the announcement of the angels. All his life, the boy longed to have a glimpse of Jesus. This is the miraculous narrative of how that happened.

j. Family members presented vocal or instrumental solos or duets. "Heirlooms," a family favorite, was often presented as a duet by our two younger daughters, Connie and Merilee. The final line says: "My precious Savior is more than an heirloom to me." Another family favorite, "Star Carol," by Alfred Burt, was typically sung by one of our daughters. Its message was one of response with the words:

"I'll make a place for Thee in my heart." One of our young adult grandsons played a piano etude by Chopin that is set to the words of a prayer, "O Speak to Me." Oldest son, Sherman, traditionally sang "O Holy Night." In more recent years, he often harmonized it with his granddaughter, Grace. Our oldest daughter, Sharon, always played her violin. Besides often playing "Meditation from Thais" by Massenet, a favored classical piece, she also played some beautiful carols with piano accompaniment. Accomplished daughter-in-law, Marti, delighted us by playing her creative "on-the-spot" Christmas medleys. We got to choose the songs for the medley! The older great grandchildren sang contemporary Christian worship songs. They always loved having a part in these Christmas presentations.

k. The evening always included everyone singing Christmas carols. We made a "joyful noise" for Jesus' birthday while the smallest great grandchildren danced around, played with balloons, rolled around on the floor under the grand piano while laughing… or crying!

l. Several times we went family Christmas caroling up and down our street. The littlest boy did his part by ringing the doorbell! Guitar accompaniment kept us up to tempo!

6. As any birthday party would only be complete with gift-giving to the honored one, so we always included gift-giving TO JESUS a very important component to our celebrations. Generally, the choices for gifts distributed "in Jesus' name," were made by each separate family in the extended clan. I share with you below several gifts choices we made during the time our four children were in our home.

   a. One of our first attempts was to give to a young minister and his family whom we thought could definitely benefit from some new and needed items. We chose to give new clothing for each person. Secretly we found out their sizes. We chose to give a white dress shirt and tie to the man, a nice dress for the woman, two play outfits for the boys, and darling, little dresses for the girls. We packaged these items in a large, beautifully wrapped box. On Christmas morning, we went as a family and placed the box on their porch with a Christmas card which read, "Your Gift in Jesus' Name." Our children have never forgotten the joy of that doorstep surprise left because we loved Jesus, the Honored One at Christmas.

b.   Another time we asked our children if they had any friends they thought were in need. Sure enough, our then teenage daughter wanted to give to a friend and her mother who lived in one room in a boarding house.

c.   Other years we decided to give toward missionaries we knew were in need or to missions projects we were made aware of through our church.

Certainly there are a host of other things that can be done to keep Christ the centerpiece of your family's celebration. Perhaps, however, I have "whetted your appetite" or "kindled the flame" to keep those "home fires burning" as you develop meaningful traditions in your family, no matter its size, shape, or stage.

*

"The Rewarding Sounds of Loving Relationships"

Every so often we hear others refer to a married couple's love as though it was "a marriage made in heaven." I am not sure just how that works, or what others have particularly in mind when they make that comment, but I do believe the dear Lord brought Sherman and me together in a sweet and remarkable way. I dreamed of having the truly "right choice" for my life partner. I recall reading a verse in the Bible that says, "If you are willing and obedient, you will eat the good things of the land." (Isaiah 1:19)

I felt that I was willing and wanted so much to be obedient to the Lord in every area of my life. So, I called upon Him to give me what was the best young man in the land--or in the Bible school I was attending! It turned out to be Sherman Williams. Hooray! He was the one!! Yes, that is where Sherman and I first met. As we were both involved in music at school, he took that common interest to find a "natural way" to approach me. He asked me if I had a copy of the song, "Give Me Thy Heart." I bent over backwards to give him a copy! We have often laughed a bit at his request. It was just a chance to speak directly to one another, for ours was a new school which had some restrictions regarding "fraternizing" between the young men and women. We were often reminded that we were in the Bible school to prepare for work in the ministry of the Gospel, not primarily to socialize with one another. We could not date unless we received special permission from the Superintendent of the school. Because of this, Sherman and I did not date unless we were on school breaks.

As it turned out, I worked for my room and board up the hill just beyond the boys' dorm. So, when I walked to school, I very conveniently passed the dorm on the other side of the street. One Valentine's Day, Sherman watched for me to go by. Out he came with a box of beautiful, long-stemmed roses. On the box was a ribbon that said, "SAY IT WITH FLOWERS." Even without formal dating, we found ways to realize and express our interest in each other. Young people do find a way!

Sherman had grown up as a farm boy, son to Sherman, Sr. and Lydia Williams, and brother to Erma and Lorraine. His dad was a farmer and car salesman. He worked with his dad at harvest time driving trucks, including a combine, and hauling grain. At a young age he also became a car salesman. Always young for his high school grade, he graduated at sixteen. As his family was very frugal, Sherman learned that was the way to live your life. This turned out to be helpful in the ministry, which was never to become a lucrative profession! BUT GOD, the great provider, always takes care of His own. He forever proved faithful to us.

At the close of high school, Sherman attended a youth rally in Spokane, Washington. His hometown, Latah, population 200, was about forty miles away. Though going to the "big city" was certainly a new and exciting experience, it was in his small farm town that he had been trained and encouraged to take an active part in his church and in special meetings in neighboring communities. He and his younger sister often sang duets, learning from an early age to give their talents to the Lord they loved. But, it was for the big youth rally in Spokane that Sherman was asked to give his first sermon. He chose as his subject the Old Testament prayer of Jabez: "'Oh, that you would bless me and enlarge my territory! Let your hand be with me, and keep me from harm so that I will be free from pain.' And God granted his request." (I Chronicles 4:10)

Following the sermon, some of the young people knelt at the altar to consecrate themselves to the work of the Lord. The elders came and placed their hands on Sherman and others, dedicating them to the Lord. This was a turning point in Sherman's life. During high school, he had thought he'd like to be an aeronautical engineer. He had made an interesting scrapbook with pictures and articles about airplanes and career associations with that in mind. However, when he preached that first sermon asking God to enlarge his ambitions, he was compelled to give himself in direct service to the Lord. He cancelled his application to the aeronautical school and enrolled at the new Northwest Bible Institute in Seattle, Washington. YES! That's where I found "My Mister Wonderful!" That's where we found each other and became life partners. As the Gospel song says, "Jesus Led Me All the Way." He faithfully led us through our many years together in pastoral and missionary-related work for our great God and Master.

I can't thank God enough for giving me the right choice for a husband, that "best young man," Sherman Williams. Never did he waver from his dedication to the Master. Never did he lose his tender heart toward God.

What a privilege it was from the time we were newlyweds and through our senior years to team up with him in ministry. Besides being a loving pastor to several congregations, I think I would term him what you might call a church entrepreneur. Offering all his God-given leadership abilities to His Lord and Savior, he not only became a visionary in the church of Christ, but also faithfully carried the vision through to completion.

As effective as he was in his work, his passion for building, encouraging and fostering a Christian home was a top priority for him. While caring for the needs of others, he was careful to love and train his own children, as well as place high value on maintaining and guarding our own love relationship as a couple.

Our family ate meals together and read the Bible (or Bible storybook) together. We made every effort to provide an "open table" and "open living room" to field questions and talk over our faith. Both Sherman and I welcomed free interaction on any subject.

Though proud of their father's accomplishments, our adult children have emphasized that his role as their available father spoke volumes to them. He took the children grocery shopping, let them comb and fuss with his hair as he read the newspaper, took them to his office, and sent them cards (with sticks of gum enclosed) while away on trips. He taught them all to drive, showed them how to treat their mother, and asked forgiveness when he spoke impatiently. He knew his children as individuals and tailored his fathering specifically to each one. Being a "shepherd dad" was as important to them, if not more so, than his being a "shepherd pastor" to congregations.

After coming home from the hospital in his last days following a stroke, he asked for the entire family to gather in our family room where we had often shared many conversations "around the fireplace." With everyone there, he gave his final blessings and soon left us for his heavenly home. Each of our four children was able to say their goodbyes, being assured of a father's faithful and consistent love throughout their lives. He was definitely the leader of our home, and was ready to pass down that leadership to his children. It was their honor to assure him of their love and their intentions to follow the Savior he loved.

I pause here to say that if you are married, continual attention to your marriage relationship is of utmost importance for the welfare and health of your family. Careers, child rearing, and even all the work associated with church ministry or service can easily distract you from the time, effort and joy in "keeping the love fires burning" in your hearts as husband and wife. Treat one another with respect. Listen well. Act in kindness. Create an atmosphere and foster your desire in understanding each other. Never take one another for granted, but seek to place the other's well being above your own. Look for new ways to express your love and hold on to the ones that you know work! Remember that there are seasons to love. Each one has its challenges and its very specific joys. Do whatever it takes to guard your hearts and minds so that you remain fully devoted to your spouse. When you come to some bumps in the road, seek advice or counsel from godly couples you can trust who are examples to you. Remember that all couples have challenges; you are not alone. And always, always count on Jesus to be the foundation of your love. He is the One who will make your house stand. He is the One who can help you weather the storms, for they will indeed come. Love with all your heart. Love without reservation. Love with purity and focused devotion. This, my married friends, will be extremely important in keeping the "home fires burning." God bless you as you look to the Founder of Marriage to keep you on His track, holy unto Him…together.

*

"P.S."

Though I have written about the Christian home from the perspective of one including both mother and father, some people reading my words may be single parents. No matter what the contour of your present family, whether you are divorced, never married, or widowed, God has a wonderful goal for your family. He desires each of us to look to Him to bring purpose, love, encouragement and a sense of belonging to our home.

God has worked with families of all kinds, from all cultures and times, who long to follow His principles and loving, wise instructions as the Creator of the family. Placing Him first, both individually and as a family, our deepest desires are fulfilled.

*

Conclusion: "My Challenge to You"

My life was like the little boy's lunch that was given to Jesus. The lunch was small and very insignificant. It was not enough for more than one boy who was following with the crowd that day long ago. But the dear Lord knew that boy was there. And, He knew about the five barley rolls and the two fish he had caught in the stream.

When I came to Jesus, all I had to offer was the scanty "little lunch" of my life— my "prairie chicken image" life. But He took it. He wanted it. Think of that! He asked me for it. I gave it to Him. "Here, Lord, is my lunch, my heart, all my life from here on out." That day He took my small lunch in His great, miracle-working hands. He blessed it, broke it, and multiplied it. He has used it to feed, can you believe it, a multitude!

Imagine, if you would, a large wicker picnic basket with a red and white gingham bow tied on the handle. It is filled with all kinds of special lunch packages—different sizes, different shapes, different contents. Each package represents the different types of lunches of our lives. I hold up a package to you and say, "Have you given the lunch of your life to Jesus? He wants it, no matter what it consists of. It may be your musical or dramatic or intellectual talents.

114

It may be your unique abilities to teach and train others. It may be your gift of helping others, your kindness, your generosity, your 'homespun' style of giving. Or, perhaps it is your willingness and availability to work at needed times and places. Whatever it is, He wants it and will use it. Mine was only a 'brown bagger' kind of lunch, but I handed it over to Jesus, and He is still multiplying it, even as I grow old. I wish that you might be willing to turn over your lunch to the Master. He will bless it, multiply it, and use it to give Him honor and praise."

The words of one of my favorite songs summarize my gratefulness for the way God has led me. I share its lyrics, my personal testimony, with you:

"Jesus Led Me All the Way"

Someday life's journey will be o'er,
And I shall reach that distant shore;
I'll sing while entering heaven's door,
"Jesus led me all the way."

Jesus led me all the way,
Led me step by step each day;
I will tell the saints and angels
As I lay my burden down,
"Jesus led me all the way."

If God should let me there review
The winding paths of life I knew,
It would be proven clear and true,
"Jesus led me all the way."

And hitherto my Lord has led,
Today He guides each path I tread,
And soon in heav'n it will be said,
"Jesus led me all the way."[6]

John W. Peterson

Epilogue

Dear Ones,

It is late in the day now. I am an old woman looking back on my life. I started my journey looking forward to my dream of having a home that would bring glory to God. I wanted to make my home one where the "home fires are still burning." At least I have tried.

I now lay down my pen.

God has helped me change my "prairie chicken image" to that of a soaring eagle, rising above my insecurities, and following His dreams for me. And, should this book have inspired you with some ideas on how to keep your "home fires burning," then I will soar into an exultation of praise to God for transforming this one prairie chicken into a bird that fulfills the purpose for which it was created. If He can do this for me, He can do it for you.

Fly! Soar! And…"keep the home fires burning!"

Thanks

How could I have done it without them?

First, there is my eldest daughter, Sharon Erickson. She was my cheerleader from the very beginning. She believed in me and helped convince me that I had something important to offer. She spent hours typing and making early edits as the book began to unfold.

Next, I want to thank my middle daughter, Connie Snyder, for shuffling through many pieces of story line and insights God had given me in order to bring cohesiveness to the project. She edited, re-edited, offered suggestions, yet always tried to remain true to my ideas and vision for the book. And then, when it all seemed to be placed together in sensible order and with clarity of purpose, she typed the final manuscript.

Thanks also goes to my grandson, Dan Erickson. From South Africa he was the chosen graphic artist, designing the book cover and providing the layout. With his artistic eye, he helped make this a truly inter-generational effort!

To many friends and more family, I am grateful for their encouragement over the years. They kept asking me, "Is your book finished yet? When it is, remember that I want a copy!"

Then I cannot neglect to thank my dear Lord for giving me the story. It was He who changed my life. He gave me inspiration for writing it down to pass on to those who might profit from His dealing with me and teaching me His ways. Without His inner prompting, I would have given up thinking that this ever could be accomplished. He spurred me on. How could I not try to follow through? Praise Him!

Notes

[1] Taken from **"The Pursuit of Excellence"** by Ted Engstrom Copyright ©1982 by Ted Engstrom. Used by permission of Zondervan. www.zondervan.com, pp. 15-16

[2] **PUT ME IN YOUR POCKET** Words and Music by DORCAS COCHRAN and HENRI RENE Copyright ©1951 (Renewed) UNICHAPPELL MUSIC INC. All Rights Reserved. Used by Permission of ALFRED MUSIC.

[3] **SOMEBODY LOVES YOU** By CHARLES TOBIAS and PETER DE ROSE © CHED MUSIC CORPORATION (ASCAP) and LARRY SPIER CO. (ASCAP) All Rights on Behalf of CHED MUSIC CORPORATION Administered by WB MUSIC CORP. All Rights Reserved

[4] Taken from **"The Pursuit of Excellence"** by Ted Engstrom Copyright ©1982 by Ted Engstrom. Used by permission of Zondervan. www.zondervan.com, p. 45

[5] Bill Drury, **"The Servant's Heart"** ©1977. Used by Permission.

[6] John W. Peterson, **"Jesus Led Me All the Way"** ©1954 John W. Peterson Company. All rights reserved. Used by permission.

Made in the USA
Charleston, SC
15 May 2015